10092
394.268

W9-BBB-636

Lower School Library
Academy of the Sacred Heart
4521 St. Charles Avenue
New Orleans, La. 70115

A HOLIDAY BOOK
Christmas in America

BY LILLIE PATTERSON

ILLUSTRATED BY VINCENT COLABELLA

Lower School Library
Academy of the Sacred Heart
4521 St. Charles Avenue
New Orleans, La. 70115

GARRARD PUBLISHING COMPANY
CHAMPAIGN, ILLINOIS

For Phyllis Whitney and Lee Wyndham
who taught me the joy of writing for children

Holiday Books are edited under
the educational supervision of

Charles E. Johnson, Ed.D.
Professor of Education
University of Georgia

T 51285

Copyright © 1969 by Lillie Patterson
All rights reserved. Manufactured in the U.S.A.
Standard Book Number 8116-6563-1
Library of Congress Catalog Card Number: 69-11077

Contents

1. Christmas Begins in America

Christmas in America today has become the merriest, cheeriest season of the year. Dazzling decorations touch everyday scenes with magical beauty. Toy departments overflow with wonders, from walking dolls to space stations. Santa Claus appears in department stores, where children whisper wishes in his ear.

The holiday spirit spreads in churches, schools, and homes. Children join in the fun of Christmas preparations—decorating homes, trimming trees, wrapping presents.

Relatives and friends arrive by cars, airplanes, and buses. "Merry Christmas!" There is the thrill of opening gifts, the joy of family feasts. There is the peace of sharing the Christmas message in songs and stories.

The first American Christmases were far different. Explorers and pioneers, far from families and homes, celebrated as best they could.

Christmas Eve, 1492, found Christopher Columbus exploring islands in the West Indies. Suddenly his flagship, the *Santa María,* ran onto rocks and began to leak. Columbus and his sailors spent Christmas Day unloading supplies from the ship. Indians from Hispaniola came with canoes and helped.

Next day, the explorers and the Indians feasted together, first aboard the *Niña,* then on the island. The Indians brought gifts of gold. Columbus left some of his men to start a colony. They named it *La Navidad,* the Spanish words for Christmas.

Later some Spanish explorers celebrated Christmas in Florida during the 1500's. Hernando De Soto and his men held religious services near today's Tallahassee, Florida's capital. There were also services at St. Augustine, the oldest city in the United States.

English fishermen and fur traders also sailed along the North American coast in the 1500's. They would celebrate Christmas with a special meal. Perhaps they feasted on a deer they had shot on shore, perhaps on a huge codfish.

The first permanent English colony was Jamestown, Virginia, founded in 1607. The first Christmas there was sad. Over half of the men had died from hunger or disease. Captain John Smith was held prisoner by Indians. There were no women in the colony yet to plan fancy feasting or gay decorations. Still, the men gathered in their crude church to hear the Christmas story.

The next Christmas was a happier one. Smith's life had been saved by Pocahontas. Many Indians had become friends with the settlers. Smith and other men, searching for food, spent the second Christmas in an Indian village. "We were never more merry, nor fed on more plenty of good Oysters, Fish, Flesh, Wild Fowl, and good bread," Smith wrote. Fowl and oysters are still popular Christmas foods.

The Virginia colony grew. Women came. Big mansions were built beside the beautiful rivers. Many colonists came from rich, fun-loving families. They brought with them their festival customs of feasting, dancing,

caroling, burning Yule logs, and holding open house. The merriment lasted until Twelfth Night, January 6, or longer. This fun was mostly for adults. However children did hang up stockings for treats from Father Christmas, the English gift-bringer.

It was a different story in New England. The Puritans passed laws forbidding a merry Christmas. This strict religious group had banned gay festivals in England. They believed these festivals had grown so merry that people forgot their religious meanings. Some families did celebrate, but in secret.

The group of Puritans called Pilgrims spent their first Christmas working hard. It was just before Christmas, 1620, that they finally chose Plymouth as the place for their colony. Christmas morning dawned cold, but fair. The men rushed ashore and began building a storehouse. All day they worked at chopping, sawing, splitting trees.

Many on their ship, the *Mayflower*, were sick. Homes and food had to be found before the weather got worse.

Other Puritans settled in Massachusetts Bay. Samuel Sewall, a Puritan preacher, described a Christmas day in his diary: "December 25, 1697. Snowy day: Shops are open and sleds come to Town with Wood and Fagots as formerly." Even schools stayed open on Christmas Day.

The "no festivals" laws were dropped in 1681. It was many years, however, before all disapproval in New England ended. Anna Green Winslow, a young Massachusetts girl, kept a diary nearly a hundred years later. "I kept Christmas at home this year, and did a very good day's work, aunt says so."

Those who settled New England made Thanksgiving their big festival. Without knowing it, they gave Christmas some of its customs and festival foods. They raised

wild turkeys and ate them instead of the traditional goose at their feasts. Indians taught them how delicious wild cranberries tasted and how to plant corn, pumpkins, and squash. These foods were used for holiday feasts.

The Pilgrims found bayberry bushes growing in New England. Bayberries are covered with a gray-green wax. The berries were boiled and the wax skimmed off to make candles. Other colonists liked these fragrant candles and used them when they had company, especially at Christmastime. Bayberry candles continue to be a popular Christmas tradition in America.

Bayberry candles when burned to the socket,
Bring friends, good fortune, and gold
    to the pocket.

Old Rhyme

2. Christmas Customs Spread

The Dutch settled New Amsterdam, later called New York, in 1625. St. Nicholas Eve, December 5, ushered in their jolly Christmas season.

St. Nicholas was a Christian Bishop who lived in the fourth century in what is now modern Turkey. He spent his life and riches helping the poor and giving gifts to children. He became the legendary gift-bringer to children in Holland and many other European countries.

The ship bringing the first Dutch settlers had a figurehead of St. Nicholas. He was made the patron of their colony.

Dutch housewives spent days making holiday cakes and cookies. Sweets were baked in the shape of St. Nicholas. Huge cookies carried his image on one side.

Children had fun at parties on St. Nicholas Eve. They wrapped small cakes in thin gold paper, called gold leaf. These made glittering gifts to honor the saint who gave away his gold to others.

Children never forgot to spread a sheet near the door of their homes. Suddenly the door would open and a shower of fruits and sweets fell onto the sheet.

A man dressed as St. Nicholas entered. He wore a long white beard, a bishop's robe and tall hat, with a staff in his hand. Sometimes he brought a helper, a little boy carrying a bag of switches. "Have you been good children?" St. Nicholas asked.

"Very good!" everyone shouted. "Please don't leave any switches here."

That night, children placed their wooden shoes near fireplaces for the gifts St. Nicholas would bring. Boys and girls were always happy when they got new skates.

Dutch families spent Christmas Day going to church, visiting, and feasting. Young and old joined skating parties on the ponds.

Twelfth Night was "Three Kings Night." Children stood three candles on the ground, one for each of the Three Kings who visited Baby Jesus. They held hands and danced around the candles. Then they jumped over them. Grownups paraded, singing from house to house. They were led by three "kings" carrying a big lighted star on a pole.

More Europeans came, settling new colonies. Swedes settled Delaware, bringing legends of Santa Lucia, their favorite saint. On St. Lucia Day, December 13, their

Christmas season began with a festival of lights. The Swedes also brought stories about the Scandinavian gift-bringers, wee elves with long beards and pointed red caps.

The Moravians, a religious group, came from Germany and decided to settle in eastern Pennsylvania. Their first building was finished on Christmas Eve. Half of it was a stable. While the settlers sang in one room, cows were mooing in the next. This reminded them of the stable in Bethlehem where Christ was born. So they christened their new settlement "Bethlehem."

Moravians keep Christmas there today much as they did in colonial days. A huge star mounted atop a mountain lights the way to the city. Wax candles glow. Bands of trombones blow to usher in the season.

Part of the Moravian Christmas Eve candle service is a Love Feast, a ceremony of brotherhood and welcome. Coffee and buns are shared together in fellowship.

There are two services, the earlier one of which is for children. They drink mild coffee. Near the end of each service, trays of lighted candles are passed around. Worshipers hold high their candles and sing to welcome Christmas.

The Germans in Pennsylvania were known as Pennsylvania Dutch. The word *Deutsch,* meaning German, was confused with "Dutch" by other settlers. Pennsylvania Dutch mothers became well known for their Christmas cookies. Families kept the cookie cutters brought from Germany.

Germans helped to bring the St. Nicholas legends to America. Their name for St. Nicholas' helper was *Pelsnichol,* meaning "Nicholas in Fur." A grownup, dressed in a fur costume and carrying a long switch, checked on children's behavior. Sometimes he came with St. Nicholas, sometimes alone.

Some Germans made the Christ Child, *Christkindl,* their gift-bringer. In America,

the word *Christkindl* became Kriss Kringle.

"Barring out the schoolmaster" was popular in many places. A few days before Christmas, pupils rushed to school early and barred the schoolhouse door. Their teacher laughingly "bought" his way in with promises—a Christmas party, fewer switchings, longer holidays, shorter lessons.

19

By the late 1700's, Christmas was being celebrated in all thirteen colonies, even New England. Although the colonies were ruled by England, the customs came from many lands. As people moved about, the customs mixed.

Christmas was happy, but far simpler than today. Celebrations centered around feasting and religious services. Friends and relatives from far off came for visits that often lasted several weeks. There was almost no gift-giving among adults. Children's gifts were small, and chiefly fruits, nuts, and sweets. What toys were given were mostly homemade.

3. Christmas with George and Martha Washington

A very special wedding took place at the end of the Christmas holidays in 1759. Martha Custis, a young widow, was married to Colonel George Washington.

Martha's mansion in Virginia glowed with Christmas lights and greenery. The bride wore a silvery dress and satin shoes with diamond buckles. Washington was handsome in a blue coat lined with red silk and gold buckles on his shoes. His dress sword hung at his side.

Washington moved his bride to Mount Vernon, his plantation on the Potomac River. Christmases in Virginia were merrier than in any other colony. And the Christmases at Mount Vernon were seasons no guest ever forgot. Each year Washington ordered fancy toys from England for Martha's son and daughter, Jacky and Patsy Custis. Presents for Jacky included a fiddle, a coach, a toy stable with horses, and a whip. Patsy enjoyed tea sets, dolls, sewing kits, and toy furniture.

The fields and woods around Mount Vernon echoed with barking dogs and galloping horses during the Christmas season. Washington's favorite sport was hunting. Neighbors and friends came to join him.

The rooms of Mount Vernon rustled with silks and satins as guests dined and danced. Martha was known for her good foods, especially cakes. The recipe for her

Christmas cake is still used. It is called a "Great Cake" and is made with 40 eggs!

Washington was well known for making good eggnog. This replaced the "wassail" drink of England. Washington would sip eggnog with guests, smile, and offer his familiar greeting: "All our friends!"

Then a change came around 1775. The American colonies began their fight for independence from England. Washington was made Commander of the American Army. On July 4, 1776, the colonies formed the United States of America.

That next Christmas, Washington and his army headed for Trenton, New Jersey. He wrote in his diary: "Christmas, 6:00 P.M. It is fearfully cold and raw, and a snowstorm setting in." He was about to make a bold move. He felt that German soldiers who were fighting with the English would be celebrating Christmas and would not be keeping patrol. Washington crossed the icy

Delaware River, took them by surprise, and won a victory.

The next few Christmases were times of hardship for Washington's army, and for many Americans. The soldiers were ragged, cold, and hungry. For Christmas dinners they had little meat, sweets, or even bread. Martha, like other housewives, knitted warm clothes for the soldiers.

Victory came in 1783. On Christmas Eve, the victorious General Washington rode home. That was one of the happiest holidays ever celebrated at Mount Vernon.

Five happy seasons passed. Washington, now a farmer again, loved the holly tree. He planted many kinds and experimented in making them more beautiful.

Holly, which grew wild along the Atlantic coast, was the most popular Christmas decoration in colonial America. Its red berries and green leaves brightened many homes. The Indians loved holly too.

They used holly as a badge of honor, just as the Romans used laurel. They drank tea made from holly leaves to give them courage in battle. Indian girls decorated their hair with holly berries.

More and more Americans planted wild holly in their yards and gardens. English holly was brought over and planted in the Pacific Northwest. The climate there is much like England's. English holly has darker, glossier leaves than American holly and more scallops and prickers. However its berries are paler. Mistletoe also grows in both Europe and America. It is used here, as there, for kissing boughs.

In 1789 George Washington stopped farming to become President of the United States. In Philadelphia, then the national capital, he and Martha gave big public receptions during the Christmas holidays. Many later American Presidents followed the Washingtons' example.

4. "Christmas Gift!"

By the early 1800's, Christmas festivals were well established in the Southern United States. The rivers, woods, and rich farmlands provided foods for grand feasts. The merrymaking was somewhat different from that held in colder Northern states, however.

On large plantations excitement began building with hog-killing time in November. Soon big turkeys were caught and fattened.

Bustling began in the kitchen of the Big House where the plantation owner lived. Fruit cakes were baked and stored away.

Woodpiles grew higher. Fires burned brighter during the Christmas season. The biggest log was saved for the Yule, or Christmas log. Evergreen boughs and holly were gathered to decorate doors, hallways, windows, mantles, and mirrors.

The best hams were brought from the smokehouse, and oysters by the barrelful were brought from the rivers. "Only the best for Christmas," was the belief.

By Christmas Eve, kinfolk and friends were arriving at the Big House. All brought their children, and many brought servants. At dusk, candles were lighted. Children hung up their stockings.

Excitement ran through the slave quarters too. Christmas Eve began a week-long holiday from hard work for most slaves. A cowbell called them to worship. Slaves

called it "Watching for the Coming of Christ." They could not read, but they knew the Christmas story well. They dearly loved the poor little baby born in a stable. At midnight they welcomed His birth with singing.

Oh, Mary, what you gonna name
That pretty little baby?
Glory, glory, glory to the new born King!
Some will call Him one thing,
But I think I'll call Him Jesus.
Glory, glory, glory to the new born King!

Plantations awoke to the firing of "Christmas guns" on Christmas morning. French settlers brought this custom to America.

Christmas guns were followed by Christmas greetings. "Christmas Gift! I surprise you!" This was an old game played between slaves and owners. If the slave gave the greeting first, he could demand a small gift. Slaves tried to surprise each other too, though they had only smiles to give as gifts. "Christmas Gift!" was passed down as a way of saying "Merry Christmas" in the South.

Families who did not live on the large plantations celebrated as happily as the rich planters, but in a simpler manner. Both rich and poor families usually served eggnog before breakfast as the first food on Christmas morning. Families and their guests went to church, if one was near enough. Church pews, decorated with evergreens, were like arbors. The Christmas feast was held about three o'clock in the afternoon.

Christmas in the South was filled with noise and excitement, much like the Fourth of July. Children played with noisy toys found in their Christmas stockings. They popped firecrackers, crackled sparklers, blew paper horns, tooted whistles, and sailed

balloons. Poor children and slave children made balloons from dried hog bladders.

In many cities young men enjoyed the medieval Christmas custom of mummering. They dressed in masks and costumes, and marched from house to house, skylarking, singing, and dancing. Wrestling matches and shooting contests were popular in cities and country places. Winners often received a goose or a turkey as a prize.

Negro slaves added one of America's charming contributions to the Christmas festival. They created religious folk songs, called spirituals, to express their feelings. Several told of their joy over the coming of the Christ Child. His birth gave them hope of freedom.

> Go, tell it on the mountain,
> Over the hills and everywhere;
> Go, tell it on the mountain,
> That Jesus Christ is born.
> *American Negro Spiritual*

5. Christmas Goes West

The United States doubled in size in 1803 when the Louisiana Territory was bought from France. French settlers spread customs of their Christmas, called *Noël*. French celebrations centered around the *crèche*, the manger scene. On Christmas Eve children knelt before a *crèche* and asked the Christ Child, *Petit Noël*, to remember them with gifts. Some families made Father Christmas, *Père Noël*, their gift-bringer.

By 1850 the United States stretched to the Pacific Ocean. Christmas moved with the explorers, fur traders, and pioneers who settled the West. These settlers in turn learned new customs from Spain and Mexico, since these countries had owned much of the Southwest.

The poinsettia, one of America's most popular Christmas plants, came from Mexico. Dr. Joel Poinsett, the first U.S. ambassador to Mexico, saw poinsettias there at Christmas time. In 1828, he sent cuttings to the United States where they grew nicely. Mexicans called the plant "Flower of the Holy Night." Some Americans named it poinsettia for Dr. Poinsett.

Fur trappers or "mountain men" in the Rockies were often lonely at Christmastime. So they invited Indians to share their Christmas dinners. Indians called Christmas "The Big Eating." These dinners included lots of meats—elk, bear, and buffalo.

French and Spanish missionaries set up missions and taught the Indians. As many as 300 Indians would come to spend Christmas week at the Mission Santa Clara in California. Orange trees hung bright with fruit. Guitars and mandolins added music to the mission bells which rang throughout the season.

Many of the Indians could not read or even speak the language of their teachers. So the priests used old folk plays to teach the Christmas Story. These plays had been used in medieval days to teach peasants who could not read. How the Indians loved acting out the Nativity! They made up many dances to retell the story.

Three of these Spanish plays have been revived in the Southwest. *Los Pastores,* The Shepherds, tells of the shepherds' visit to Bethlehem to honor the Christ Child. *Los Tres Reyes Magos,* The Three Wise Men, tells of the three kings' gifts.

Las Posadas, the Lodgings, acts out the journey of Mary and Joseph and their search for lodging. The play lasts nine nights, since legends say that Mary and Joseph traveled nine days to Bethlehem, and ends on Christmas Eve.

The West developed rapidly after gold was discovered in California in 1848. Gold miners would stop their digging and honor Christ's birthday with a gay "Christmas jollification." The men beat out tunes with their gold-digging tools and pans while they danced and sang.

Texans joined many other western settlers in developing big cattle ranches. Lonely cowboys celebrated with Christmas dances. Some of them took the part of "lady" dancers by tying handkerchiefs around their arms. Lumberjacks in the Northwest had similar parties.

European immigrants helped to settle the West. Scandinavians brought their custom

of feeding the birds at Christmastime. They set out grain atop tall poles in snow-filled yards. Children today still make Christmas trees for birds by hanging bits of bread or seeds on branches.

Farm families on the prairies were often snowed-in for Christmas. They worried if the presents, ordered from a catalog, would arrive on time. However, like farm families everywhere, they made most of their gifts themselves. Even young children sewed, knitted, hammered, or whittled gifts.

Sleighing parties were popular, as they were in the Northeast. Teenagers wrapped in buffalo robes skimmed over the prairies in "cutters" built for two. And the younger children rode in hay-filled sleighs, singing to the gay jingle of the sleigh bells:

> Jingle bells! Jingle bells!
> Jingle all the way!
> Oh, what fun it is to ride
> In a one-horse open sleigh!

6. Santa Claus

The story of Santa Claus developed in exciting chapters. When the English took over New Amsterdam, their children found the Dutch St. Nicholas more colorful than Father Christmas. They "adopted" St. Nicholas, but had him come on Christmas Eve as Father Christmas had done.

In 1809 Washington Irving published a story about New York called *Knickerbocker's History*. In it, he described the St. Nicholas

Festival. Until then, everyone thought of the gift-bringer as a saintly figure. Irving described him as a fun-loving, pipe-smoking man, riding across rooftops in a wagon with gifts for children.

The book was read throughout the country. Soon St. Nicholas began to take the place of the old gift-bringers.

Clement Clarke Moore, a New York City professor, read *Knickerbocker's History*. On Christmas Eve, 1822, he told his children, "I must go downtown to buy the Christmas turkey."

"Bring us a Christmas surprise!" they called back.

As the sleigh skimmed along the snowy streets, Moore wondered what treat he could give his children. Suddenly he decided: a surprise poem! While sleigh bells jingled, he created the lines in his head. That night, he gathered his children about him and recited:

'Twas the night before Christmas,
    when all through the house
Not a creature was stirring,
    not even a mouse;
The stockings were hung by the chimney
    with care,
In hopes that St. Nicholas
    soon would be there . . .

Moore's Santa was "dressed all in fur, from his head to his foot," like the German *Pelsnichol*. He had the pipe, twinkling eyes, and rosy cheeks of the Dutch settlers. He was chubby and fat, but "a right jolly old elf."

Earlier pictures and poems had given Santa one reindeer. Moore gave him eight, and named them Dasher and Dancer, Prancer and Vixen, Comet and Cupid, Donder and Blitzen.

The poem was printed in a newspaper and called "An Account of a Visit from St. Nicholas."

The popular Dutch name for St. Nicholas was *Sinter Klaas*. English children tried to say this and excitedly said "Santa Claus."

An illustration in 1843 showed Santa dressed in a fur coat with a bishop's cross on his cap. Another in 1847 pictured him wearing fur-trimmed clothes, high boots, and a feather in his cap. Thomas Nast, a young cartoonist from Germany, created the Santa we know today.

In 1863, Nast drew Santa for *Harper's Weekly* magazine. Santa was dressed in the Stars and Stripes, giving gifts to soldiers in a Civil War camp. Nast illustrated Santa again, changing him a little each time.

In 1866, the present Santa emerged. Santa has the white beard of Father Christmas and St. Nicholas. He wears the red color of St. Nicholas' robe, fur from *Pelsnichol,* and the peaked cap of the Scandinavian elves. Santa's pipe, jolly looks, and his plumpness come from the Dutch.

7. The Christmas Tree

The Christmas tree grew popular during the 1800's. The custom began in Germany and was brought to America by soldiers during the Revolutionary War. But the idea did not catch on at first.

Two German teachers, Charles Follen and Charles Minnegerode, helped to popularize the custom. Follen, who was a teacher in Cambridge, Massachusetts, had enjoyed Christmas trees as a boy in Germany. Each year after 1832, he trimmed one for his young son and invited other children to enjoy it.

Minnegerode came from Germany in 1842 to teach in Williamsburg, Virginia. That Christmas he trimmed a tree for the children of another teacher. He taught the children how to string popcorn and loop the strings over the branches. They added round balls made of colored paper and painted nuts. Candles were fastened to the branches with wires, and a star was placed on top.

In 1850 an American magazine printed a picture of the British Royal family around their first Christmas tree. It had been decorated by German-born Prince Albert, Queen Victoria's husband. The picture of this tree caught the fancy of the American people. Also, thousands of Germans came to America during the mid-1800's and spread the custom faster.

President Franklin Pierce set up the first Christmas tree in the White House in 1856. He invited some Sunday school children to come and sing around it. Sunday schools began using Christmas trees in the 1850's and helped to popularize them. Children saw the pretty trees in church and wanted one at home.

Early Christmas tree decorations were mostly homemade. There were sweets— sugarplums, gingerbread men, cookies, and candy canes. Apples, oranges, and lemons made bright balls. Children had fun stringing cranberries and popcorn. They also made cotton balls for snow, paper chains, and painted eggshells and nuts. Tiny horns and tin soldiers hung from branches. Small American flags were popular tree decorations in the 1860's.

Families set up Christmas trees in front parlors, used for special company. Children, dressed in their best, marched in to sing

around the lighted trees. Someone always held a wet sponge fastened to a stick to put out fires if a candle tipped over.

Ralph E. Morris, a New England telephone company worker, watched the small signal bulbs light up telephone switchboards. "They are just right for lighting trees safely," he said. He strung electric light bulbs on his family's tree in 1895. Electric lights made trees more dazzling and more popular.

Moravian families have always placed a manger scene, or *Putz,* under or near their Christmas trees. The name *Putz* is from the German word meaning "to decorate." A *Putz* usually includes things that tell of the life of the people. Tiny mountains, farms, animals, and even creeks can be part of the scene.

Decorations are saved and passed down to children. Friends go *Putz*-visiting to see which homes have the prettiest scenes.

Out-of-town visitors come to see the big community *Putz* set up by the Moravian Church.

Germans brought the *Putz* idea to Baltimore. There, they are known as Christmas Gardens.

Santa Claus and the Christmas tree helped make Christmas more of a children's festival. They also made gift-giving more popular, especially among adults. Santa's toys became bigger and fancier, as hundreds of toyshops and toymakers sprang up in the United States.

Christmas tree farms became a big business, too. The fir, pine, and spruce are favorite trees. Early on Christmas morning, children rush to see all the presents piled beneath them. Today, as in the 1800's, a sled is a popular present in much of the United States.

8. A Season of Good Will

"There is no peace on earth," Longfellow wrote in a Christmas poem during the Civil War. Christmases during the war years were sad. Many husbands and fathers were in the armies. Food was costly and scarce, especially in the South. Near the end of the war a turkey cost as much as $100. Candy cost eight dollars a pound. Many families cooked Christmas dinners, then gave them away to hungry soldiers.

51

Mothers tried to give children a happy Christmas. This was not easy. Santa Claus was very popular in both North and South. Children hopefully hung up stockings, only to find them empty Christmas morning.

In spite of these hardships, Christmas customs continued to flourish. People seemed to need the Christmas message more than ever.

American authors wrote stories as well as poems about wartime Christmases. Louisa May Alcott nursed wounded soldiers in a hospital. She wrote a story about them called "A Hospital Christmas."

She wrote about Christmas in many later books. *Little Women* is about her own family in Massachusetts. One chapter tells how the four sisters, Meg, Jo, Beth, and Amy, learn of a poor woman whose children are hungry. Though they, too, are poor, the girls pack their Christmas breakfast and give it to the family.

Charles Dickens visited the United States in 1867, two years after the war ended. He traveled about, reading from his famous stories. On Christmas Eve, he read from *A Christmas Carol*.

This story tells of Scrooge, a rich old miser, who feels that Christmas celebrations are wasteful. One Christmas Eve he has a frightful dream. He is visited by three ghosts: Christmas Past, Christmas Present, and Christmas Yet to Come. The dream teaches Scrooge the joy of Christmas giving. "I will honor Christmas in my heart and try to keep it all the year," he declares. Dickens' readings made Christmas even more popular than before.

A Christmas Carol still reminds Americans of the true spirit of Christmas. President Franklin D. Roosevelt read the story to his children and grandchildren each Christmas Day. Many other families share it each year, and children dramatize it in schools.

The Christmas card custom spread this spirit of good will across America. Louis Prang is called "Father of the American Christmas Card." Prang came penniless from Germany and opened a small print shop in Massachusetts. He perfected a way of making colored pictures cheaply and began selling Christmas cards in 1875. The first cards were small and printed on one side. By 1900 American Christmas cards were bigger, more beautiful, and more popular. Today they are a big industry.

Christmas cards are often brightened by Christmas seals. Einar Holboell, a postal clerk in Denmark, got the idea while stamping Christmas mail in 1903. There could be a Christmas stamp to help sick people! Others agreed. The first seals were sold in Denmark in 1904 and in the United States in 1907. Money from seals is used to help stamp out tuberculosis and other diseases.

9. Carols and Caroling

Caroling has always been one of the joys of the American Christmas. Many of the carols were brought from Europe.

During the 19th century Americans added lovely carols of their own. Some of the best were written by ministers. Most carols were written as poems and later set to music.

One of the earliest was written by Reverend Edmund Sears of Massachusetts.

One December day in 1850, he watched the peaceful scene of snow covering the countryside. Reverend Sears thought of the first Christmas when a Babe brought peace to the world. He put his hopes and prayers in a poem, "It Came Upon the Midnight Clear."

One of the few carols about the visit of the Wise Men is "We Three Kings of Orient Are." The Reverend John Henry Hopkins, Jr. wrote the words and music in 1857 while a minister in Pennsylvania. Children enjoy dramatizing it in school and church. There are verses for each King and verses for singing together.

> O star of wonder, star of night,
> Star with royal beauty bright,
> Westward leading, still proceeding,
> Guide us to the perfect light.

Bishop Phillips Brooks loved children and wrote his carols especially for them. He visited the Holy Land in 1865 and spent Christmas Eve in Bethlehem. The sight of the little town in the moonlight filled him with wonder. After he returned to America, he painted the scene with words and music. The gentle carol, "O Little Town of Bethlehem," was first sung by children of his Sunday school in 1868.

During the 20th century, outdoor caroling grew very popular. The section of Boston called Beacon Hill became famous for caroling. Sometimes the carolers dress in ancient costumes and carry old lanterns or shepherd's crooks. Some ring handbells.

The 71 bells in the Bok Singing Tower, atop Iron Mountain in Florida, ring carols each Christmas. In places along the Pacific coast, carolers sing from beautifully lighted boats. In York, Pennsylvania, the factory whistles toot carols on Christmas Eve.

Radio, television, and records bring carols to everyone throughout the season.

10. Christmas in Modern America

Christmas was a legal holiday in all the states by the end of the 19th century. The customs borrowed from Europe have blended with America's contributions to make a colorful, exciting holiday.

One of America's chief contributions is the community Christmas tree. Cities and towns, as well as families, decorate outdoor trees. Many places are famous for their Christmas tree traditions.

The National Christmas Tree is decorated on the White House lawn. The President pushes a button to light the towering tree in a special ceremony. Each year he broadcasts a Christmas message to the nation.

A few weeks before Christmas, a giant tree is decorated in Rockefeller Center in New York City. Visitors from all over the country come to see its beauty and to hear the caroling around it.

A redwood in central California is called the "Nation's Christmas Tree." This tree, over 3,000 years old, was growing at the time Christ was born. Each Christmas, worshipers of different faiths hold services at its base.

Altadena, California boasts a "Christmas Tree Lane." The graceful cedars were brought from India. Visitors drive by, car lights dimmed, to see the wonder of 200 lighted trees.

Strangely, Christmas customs seem to spread and grow stronger during wars. American soldiers have introduced Christmas trees, caroling, Santa Claus, and turkey to people in far-away places. One soldier painted flashlight bulbs to decorate a tree on a South Pacific island during World War II. The headlights of jeeps were turned on the tree, while men caroled around it in the jungle night.

The United States added two new states, Alaska and Hawaii, in the 1950's. They brought with them new Christmas customs. Santa Claus comes to Alaska riding down the snow-covered main street in a sled drawn by a team of huskies. He sometimes appears with live reindeer!

Santa arrives on the beach at Waikiki to open the Christmas season in Hawaii. He paddles a canoe or rides a surfboard. The beaches are joyful with caroling to the music of guitars and ukuleles.

Christmas dinner in Hawaii is often an outdoor feast called a luau. Roast pig is served side by side with turkey, and eggnog with pineapple punch.

Christmas customs differ in parts of America, as in other places throughout the world. Still, the meanings behind them are the same. The American Christmas remains a religious festival, honoring the birthday of Christ. Colorful folk customs serve to make it gay. Gift-giving expresses people's love. Christmas is a festival that can be enjoyed by everyone, regardless of religious beliefs.

The joys and traditions of the season bring people closer together in a spirit of friendship and good will. This is as it should be. Above all, Christmas is a season of brotherhood. The angels sang of this on the first Christmas. We must sing of it today.